Scenes and Revelations

A DRAMA

by

Elan Garonzik

SAMUEL FRENCH, INC.
45 WEST 25TH STREET   NEW YORK 10010
7623 SUNSET BOULEVARD HOLLYWOOD 90046
LONDON   TORONTO

SCENES AND REVELATIONS

Scenes and Revelations had its world premier at Chicago's Goodman Theatre on March 18, 1979; artistic director, Gregory Mosher. The production was directed by Betsy Carpenter; set by James Guenther; costumes by Jessica Hahn; lights by Robert Christen. The cast was as follows:

HELENA	Susan Dafoe
CHARLOTTE	Sonja Lanzener
MILLIE	Janice St. John
REBECCA	Nan Wade
THE MAN	Tim Halligan
UNCLE JACOB	David Chadderdon
MR. KARONK	David Chadderdon

It had its New York premier off-Broadway at the Production Company in March, 1981; artistic director, Norman Rene. The production was directed by Sheldon Epps; set by Jane Thurn; costumes by Oleksa; lights by William Armstrong. The cast was as follows:

HELENA	Sofia Landon
CHARLOTTE	Caitlin O'Heany
MILLIE	Marilyn McIntyre
REBECCA	Valerie Mahaffey
THE MAN	Stephen Burleigh
UNCLE JACOB	Richard Merrell
MR. KARONK	Nicholas Saunders

It was produced on Broadway by Circle in the Square, opening in June, 1981; artistic director, Theodore Mann; managing director, Paul Libin. The production was directed by Sheldon Epps; set by Jane Thurn;

costumes by Oleksa; lights by William Armstrong. The cast was as follows:

HELENA	Christine Lahti
CHARLOTTE	Mary-Joan Negro
MILLIE	Marilyn McIntyre
REBECCA	Valerie Mahaffey
THE MAN	Norman Snow
UNCLE JACOB	Joseph Warren
MR. KARONK	Nicholas Saunders

Scenes and Revelations received the Marc Klein, Carmel, Audrey Wood and Omaha Community Playhouse playwriting awards.

To A.W.

4

CHARACTERS

(listing the four Longnecker sisters first)

HELENA—*age 26, the eldest . . . joyous, sharp, passionate*
CHARLOTTE—*age 25, a nurse . . . reserved, attentive, clear*
MILLIE—*age 23, an artist . . . bohemian and confused in love*
REBECCA—*age 19, the baby of the family . . . spirited*
THE MAN (playing the following roles)
    SAMUEL—*the farm's manager . . . sexual, self-confident*
    PETER MARTIN—*Rebecca's husband*
    DR. ZEIGLER—*for whom Charlotte worked*
    DENNIS HOUSER—*the boy on the neighboring farm . . . honest and full of charm*
UNCLE JACOB—*the sisters' uncle in Manchester, England . . . an industrialist*
MR. KARONK—*the man taking the sisters to their ship*

TIME: *September, 1894 and years earlier.*

PLACE: *The Longnecker farm in Lancaster County, Pa., and various other locations including Nebraska and Manchester, England.*

There is no intermission; the playing time is an hour and thirty-five minutes.

5

SCENES—for director's and actors' use *only*

1. Main sitting room—*the present*
2. REBECCA's bedroom—2 years prior to the present
3. DR. ZEIGLER's office—2 years prior to the present
4. Nebraska—1½ years prior to the present
5. Main sitting room—*the present*
6. Near the pond—7 years prior to the present
7. Nebraska—3 months prior to the present
8. Main sitting room—2½ months prior to the present
9. The cemetery—6 years prior to the present
10. The raspberry patch—4 months prior to the present
11. Main sitting room—*the present*
12. Near the pond—1 year prior to the present
13. Nebraska and Manchester, England—3 months prior
14. The raspberry patch—2 months prior to the present
15. Downtown—11 months prior to the present
16. Main sitting room—*the present*
17. REBECCA's bedroom—3 weeks prior to the present
18. The back porch—a few hours after scene 17
19. Main sitting room—*the present*

Scenes and Revelations

SCENE ONE

There is no curtain, and the set is comprised of a wooden rake and slight elevations connected by steps. The set should have a clean, sparce "dance" look, but should also support the inherent lyricism of the script. Upstage, there may be a overhanging eave, or the suggestion of a porch or a white picket fence. Simplicity is the rule, for the set and costumes and absolutely everything; there should be nothing on the stage that is not essential to the action. The sisters may sit on the steps.

Costumes must be unrealistic and stylized, giving the hint of the period with none of the cumbersome details. With each sister spanning a 6 year period in the play, and these being the years from youth to womanhood, realistic costumes will not work. The women's costumes should be feminine, theatrical and handsome; REBECCA's costume should be cream white, giving the hint of a wedding gown. The skirts should be a variation on one design, tying in back to give a sense of fullness; leotard will suffice for the torso. All four sisters are attractive.

Regarding transitions, much of the play is dependent on flow. It should be played without a single blackout. Scenes should be dovetailed, smoothed over by cross fades and the prior or immediate entrance of characters for the following scene. Music only before

7

*scenes in the present, to point them up. Keep the pace
going, and the audience will put the play together.*

As the lights rise, the sisters are in place. HELENA,
downright with REBECCA *beside her.* CHARLOTTE,
right center. MILLIE, *left center.*

HELENA. I wrote him. I said one o'clock. Everything
on the front porch, everything ready.

MILLIE. Do you want me to go stand outside?

HELENA. (*smiling*) No. He can find us in here.

MILLIE. (*lightening the mood*) I packed up all my
paintings. All but my sketchbook. Paintings of the
farm, the house. Things I did several years back. Millie
Longnecker. *Quelle artiste.*

HELENA. Samuel?

MILLIE. No. How strange. I never thought to paint
Samuel.

CHARLOTTE. Rebecca, child, dearest, we don't know
how to comfort you.

MILLIE. You're all being utterly maudlin. Just how
bad will Manchester be?

HELENA. No-one said—

REBECCA. (*cuts her off*) I was . . . I was married in
this house. (*pause, a moment, they let it drop*)

MILLIE. I just went through them very quickly. I
picked and chose and said: keep this, toss that, color's
bad, toss that. I won't know, until we get to England
and unpack everything—I won't know what I actually
kept. Millie-Millie—*Quelle artiste.*

(SAMUEL *enters from upright, pauses, looks at the women, then talks. He is tall, vital, athletic and handsome and is dressed in tailored comfort: boots,
brown suit, open shirt. This one costume must be*

readily adapted to his other characters with the addition or subtraction of a vest, coat, etc.)

SAMUEL. May I—excuse me—may I come in?

MILLIE. (*simply delighted*) I-knew-it-my-instinct-told-me! A farewell party!

SAMUEL. Just one, Millie. Hardly a party. (*She goes to greet him, holds his hand.*)

MILLIE. It doesn't matter. Isn't this marvelous?—look who's come wish us goodbye. Here the four of us were sitting so solemn—

CHARLOTTE. We were resting—

MILLIE. And now we've a farewell party!

SAMUEL. Of one. I saw all your trunks on the front porch. And I—actually, I can only stay a minute. But I knew you were leaving today. And—

MILLIE. Oh, can't you stay? Just until our man arrives.

SAMUEL. I'm afraid not.

HELENA. Millie, please. Samuel said he's got things to do. (*turns to him for the first time*) We've been here two weeks, packing, getting ready. It's unfortunate you've come now. At this moment. Right when we're ready to leave.

SAMUEL. But you told me—

HELENA. I didn't think you'd really believe me.

SAMUEL. Well I did.

HELENA. I thought, when we got to Manchester . . .

SAMUEL. You thought you'd write.

HELENA. Something like that.

SAMUEL. Well I won't be here. I'm leaving. Today, Helena. For California.

CHARLOTTE. (*filling in*) As she said, Samuel, this is most unfortu—

HELENA. Charlotte, please.

SAMUEL. I wasn't even going to come, you know. I'd

quite made up my mind just to leave. No goodbyes, no handshakes. I mean you asked me not to come back. But I couldn't do that. What I mean to say, Helena—is—

HELENA. Do you know how cruel this is?

SAMUEL. And yourself? I want you to know, Helena, I want you to know why I'm going to California.

MILLIE. (*suddenly stands up, hand over stomach, takes a few steps upright to exit, then turns*) I'm—I'm going out. I don't have to watch this. May I—may I be excused? Please?

SAMUEL. (*moves toward her*) I'm sorry, Millie.

MILLIE. Don't be sorry. It's just that—it's just—all my life . . . all I ever really wanted was—(SAMUEL *takes her hand and holds it very tight*.) Helena sold the farm. To the Housers—can you imagine that? I mean of all the people in the world to sell it to—(*decides it's best to drop this*)—Samuel, you were the best farm manager we ever had. Helena always said that. It's too late now, but I should've painted you. We were kindred spirits of sorts. (*kisses him lightly*) I mean California.

SAMUEL. Goodbye, Millie. Miss Charlotte, I hope you've a safe trip.

CHARLOTTE. You were, as Millie just said, you were the best.

SAMUEL. Helena?

HELENA. Things came apart. What can I say? We'd such different lives, such different things holding on-to us.

SAMUEL. Goodbye.

REBECCA. I don't want anyone sleeping in my room please. (HELENA *turns to* REBECCA.)

SAMUEL. Helena.

REBECCA. Not in my bedroom. Not mine.

HELENA. Rebecca, we've nothing to say on the matter. (SAMUEL *pauses, then exits*.)

REBECCA. I was married in this house.

HELENA. Yes, Rebecca. But you must put all that—we're going to England. Uncle Jacob's—and you'll have the best of—Charlotte, Millie, please! (*She crosses away.*)

CHARLOTTE. Rebecca, you'll have the best of everything. Uncle Jacob left us so much money. Clothes, travel—

REBECCA. (*cuts her off*) I'd wanted to go west.

HELENA. Oh, Millie, please.

MILLIE. Rebecca. Rebecca, listen to me. In England we'll become lady financiers. From behind large oak desks we'll order people about: Do this, do that! We'll smoke pipes and have powerful men address us, "Madamoiselle." We'll become adept at figures, doubling our legacy in five years, tripling it in eight. A hundred looms will become five hundred. And at the end, grey-haired, matronly, benefactress of the poor, and the very terror of the textile trade—church elders and councilmen will address me, "Madamoiselle." And I'll sternly command them, "Madame!" (*We immediately hear* PETER MARTIN *calling out* REBECCA's *name. The girls turn their heads toward his voice, and we are into the next scene. No pause.*)

SCENE TWO

(REBECCA'S *wedding day.*)

PETER MARTIN. (*calls from offright*) Rebecca Longnecker! Rebecca Longnecker!! You best get a move on! Or I'm going to honeymoon with my horse!

REBECCA. (*screams back at him*) Go off with your

horse, you ugly thing! (*looks at* CHARLOTTE) Oh, why did I say that?—I love him.

PETER MARTIN. (*off*) Helena! Millie!!

MILLIE. (*calls off*) She'll be out in a minute! She loves you!

REBECCA. No I don't! (*Her sisters prepare to send her off, fiddling with her hair, dress, etc.*)

HELENA. Honestly! You'd think he'd allow us a minute alone.

REBECCA. Alone? I've been alone all my life! Why do you think I got married?

CHARLOTTE. I thought because you love him.

REBECCA. Of course I love him. Oh, I'm so nervous I could scream.

MILLIE. Go ahead! I'll scream with you.

CHARLOTTE. There are people downstairs!

REBECCA. (*holding her head in her hands*) I'm married!—I can't believe it! Little Rebecca Longnecker's going from you all.

CHARLOTTE. To a man that loves you.

REBECCA. (*tearing at her hair*) I feel sick all of a sudden.

CHARLOTTE. Rebecca! You'll mess up your hair!

HELENA. Then he won't want to take you with him.

REBECCA. I don't care! I don't!

HELENA. (*pulling* REBECCA *up to face her*) Child, child look at me. You're just a perfect dream.

REBECCA. Am I?

MILLIE. There she goes again—begging for compliments.

REBECCA. I only beg 'cause I don't know how to get them. I'm the prettiest of the Longnecker sisters. But I'm also the stupidest. Have anymore gifts arrived?

HELENA. (*giving her a light tap on her rear*) You're terrible. Just terrible!

REBECCA. Oh, forgive me, forgive me—I'm just so confused. Maybe this was all a mistake.

HELENA. Child, calm yourself.

REBECCA. Yes, yes, it's a mistake. He's going to hate me for the rest of my life. I know—'cause I'm going to hate him!

CHARLOTTE. (*aiding her with her hair*) Rebecca, he loves you.

REBECCA. How do you know?

MILLIE. Get her out of here! Get her out of our lives!

REBECCA. (*faces* HELENA) Is my hair all right? Oooooo, why did I ever say yes? He was down on his knees like some perfect fool so sweet and boyish. Now what was I to say?

PETER MARTIN. (*calls in*) Heh, you in there! Rebecca! I'm running off with my horse!

REBECCA. (*calls off*) Oh hush up!

MR. MARTIN. You asked for it!

REBECCA. (*runs to the door*) No, no! I love you!

HELENA. Rebecca, get some control of yourself.

REBECCA. You're right, you're—all of you—oh, I love you. Will you write me?

MILLIE. Write you? Is there a P.O. in Nebraska?

REBECCA. (*drawing out the "a" and breaking from them*) Nebraska!—why in god's name does he want to take me to Nebraska?

CHARLOTTE. Because it's West, that's why! This whole country's moving West!

HELENA. And we've got to go with them. Like father did from England.

CHARLOTTE. Why, in no time all four of us will be married. Millie's going next, I can tell. Yes, yes, Dennis Houser's got fine eyes for courting Millie!

MILLIE. (*girlishly shocked*) He's hardly courting.

REBECCA. (*running to* MILLIE) Millie, do you mean it? Try and catch the flowers when I throw them!

HELENA. (*bringing* REBECCA *back*) We'll all be married soon. Don't you worry about your three older sisters! Then we'll just have to sell the farm—And move West.

MILLIE. Farther West than Nebraska. Nebraska'll be *East* of us.

REBECCA. Oh, no! Please don't sell it! I always want it here—to come back to. I love you, I do! Now listen. When we get to Nebraska I'll write you every little thing. What his sister's farm's like, what her house is like. Every little thing. I promise! Every day!

PETER MARTIN. (*calls from offstage*) Three seconds, Rebecca! Or I'm going off with my horse! ONE!

REBECCA. (*running from sister to sister, kissing them*) I love you, I love you. I love all of you, I do!

HELENA. (*as she's kissed*) Child, we're coming down with you!

PETER MARTIN. TWO!!!

REBECCA. (*more kissing*) I'll write you. I promise! Every day! Will you write me?

PETER MARTIN. THREE!!!

REBECCA. (*runs out right*) Here comes your horse! (*All sisters exit except* CHARLOTTE. *The lights cross fade for the following scene as* DR. ZEIGLER *enters. He is a mildly pompous person, wears a dark suit almost completely covered by a large white coat.*)

SCENE THREE

(*We are in* DR. ZEIGLER'S *office.*)

DR. ZEIGLER. You performed admirably today, Nurse Charlotte. Any other woman would have—

CHARLOTTE. Would have gotten ill?

DR. ZEIGLER. Yes.

CHARLOTTE. Thank you, Doctor Zeigler. Although I

hardly take pride in my stamina.

DR. ZEIGLER. It's a prerequisite. To the profession, I mean.

CHARLOTTE. You've trained me well, doctor. I suppose I've found my stamina in yours.

DR. ZEIGLER. You know they've accepted a woman at Penn Medical. In a few years she'll be a doctor, and I imagine—because Penn accepted her—quite a fine one.

CHARLOTTE. (*helps him with his coat*) Well. Looks like we're done for today.

DR. ZEIGLER. Are you chosing to ignore me? (*pause*) Very well then.

CHARLOTTE. I'm *not* ignoring you, doctor. I'm merely trying to figure you out.

DR. ZEIGLER. (*takes off his apron*) Figure me out? Charlotte, there is not much to figure out.

CHARLOTTE. Two weeks ago you mentioned Dr. Gunzler needed another nurse. And added he pays better than you. Last week you let drop that Columbia Medical is opening up a school for nurses. And today you imply I should become a doctor.

DR. ZEIGLER. I implied no such thing.

CHARLOTTE. You did.

DR. ZEIGLER. Charlotte, please. I don't want to argue with you. If I said you should study doctoring—well, then, what harm's in it. Anyway, I did not say it.

CHARLOTTE. You did!

DR. ZEIGLER. I'm going home. I don't have to listen to this. (*turns to exit.*)

CHARLOTTE. (*stops him*) No! You implied it. And I want to know why.

DR. ZEIGLER. Quite simply, I believe you'd make a fine doctor. Because you and your sisters are Anglican, you may not be able to set up practice here. Mennonites prefer Mennonite doctors. But you'll find practice somewhere. And be a fine doctor. Does that suffice you?

CHARLOTTE. No. No, it doesn't. I want to know why—precisely why!—over the past few weeks you've said everything tactful you could to get rid of me. Why?

DR. ZEIGLER. I'm not trying to get rid of you.

CHARLOTTE. You are!

DR. ZEIGLER. May we discuss this tomorrow? (*turns again*)

CHARLOTTE. (*moves from him, starts to cry*) Please stop trying to get rid of me. Please!

DR. ZEIGLER. Charlotte? (*crosses to her*) Charlotte, please. (*He touches her. They move to embrace. And kiss. He breaks away.*) I'm sorry. I never—

CHARLOTTE. Adam?

DR. ZEIGLER. I asked Dr. Gunzler to hold his position for you. I told him you'd be available.

CHARLOTTE. Adam, why are you—

DR. ZEIGLER. I don't think you should call me Adam —I think . . . Charlotte, I'd never leave my church. And they'd never accept you. Not for reason of marriage. Don't you see, Charlotte, we could never marry. I'm sorry. I never meant to hurt you. I'm—I'm going. Will you be in tomorrow?

CHARLOTTE. I don't—

DR. ZEIGLER. Dr. Gunzler wants—

CHARLOTTE. I know.

DR. ZEIGLER. The four of you—you're so different I'm trying to say we're all mostly Germanic and plain.

CHARLOTTE. Just leave. Please. No, I won't be in tomorrow.

DR. ZEIGLER. I'm sorry. I—(*He exits.* REBECCA *enters for the following scene. As the lights cross fade to spot* REBECCA, CHARLOTTE *exits.*)

SCENE FOUR

(*We are in Nebraska on a cloudless and cool day, and* REBECCA *is full of confidence and spirit.*)

REBECCA. My dear, dearer, dearest sisters! Well, I wake up each morning and I still say to myself: This is Nebraska and this is my new husband! Those two words, I assure you, weren't past of my working vocabulary nine months ago. But they certainly are now! If I wake up thinking of those words, my life is so exhorbitantly busy I've little time to dawdle the rest of the day. Let me say but this: Nebraska isn't Lancaster county. Peter has this dream. He says that thirty or forty years from now, people will turn to us from their carriages and sidewalks and streetlamps—look back— and thank us! Thank us for settling . . . this place! Oh, how I'd love to see Lancaster's sidewalks again! I must make a mischievous confession to you all—but I'm secretly hoping to get pregnant—and fast! At least when I'm with child I can feign illness every now and then—And get a rest! Another confession I must make is—when I wake up, I roll over and ask myself just who is this thing beside me. I mean nothing, absolutely nothing in my childhood prepared me for . . . married life. But I do love him so! As you can tell from the envelope, we're still residing at my sister-in-law's. Peter assures me that someday we'll purchase a farm of our own. Well that someday had better come *soon.* Helena, did you send me the blue cotton I asked for? Don't be naughty! And don't forget I'm still the baby in the family. You really must attend to me as I've so much to attend to here. I send you the greatest amount of love and hugs and kisses I can fit in this envelope. Your sister, your baby, Rebecca! (*The lights cross fade. Music announcing another scene in the present.* HELENA, CHARLOTTE *and* MILLIE *join* REBECCA *onstage.*)

SCENE FIVE

(*We are once again in the present.*)

CHARLOTTE. There was something we did last week I hope never to do again in my life.

HELENA. Clearing out the house?

CHARLOTTE. All the dolls, each piece of doll furniture. The clothes, toys—

HELENA. We should've had a great clearing out. Right when mother died.

CHARLOTTE. And been so cruel? To father?

HELENA. That's what killed him you know. Two years. Moping about the house. I'm surprised—

CHARLOTTE. Surprised at what?

HELENA. He lasted two years after mother.

CHARLOTTE. You've become, over the past years— I don't know.

REBECCA. I remember being a young girl . . . Walking in the fields. The corn. I remember pumpkins in autumn. Kicking them. Or watching your step so you don't kick them. Snapping off tobacco leaves. There's something about the earth. I remember growing oats. Going out to the field. Everyday. Checking for bugs. Or disease.

MILLIE. We never grew oats here, did we?

REBECCA. Oh, yes.

MILLIE. That's wheat you're thinking of, Rebecca. Or corn.

CHARLOTTE. (*calmly, to change the subject*) You never paid any attention anyway, Millie. Always dabbling. Always flirting with every farmhand Helena—

MILLIE. I never—

REBECCA. We grew oats! I remember praying they'd see the surface! Then praying every day: No storm— no hail—Can we get to harvest?—Can we?

MILLIE. No, Rebecca, we never grew—(REBECCA *rises and rushes upstage.*)

HELENA. Thank you. Thank you, my lovelies. Millie, please take Rebecca outside. Get your stylus or charcoals or something—and busy that artistic little head of yours.

MILLIE. Well when's Mr. Karonk going to arrive?

HELENA. That's hardly the point.

MILLIE. Anything. Anything to keep me from thinking. Is that it?

HELENA. Oh, please!

MILLIE. Oh, please! It'll all go away with a simple "please"—won't it? Oh, please!! (MILLIE *storms upstage, gets* REBECCA *and exits.*)

HELENA. Maybe you were right. Maybe I should have never allowed her to go off to Philadelphia. After all, what did she learn. All she learned was to come back.

CHARLOTTE. You've become, over the years—you've become hard.

HELENA. Why don't you knit something for Rebecca. A sweater. It'll give her something to look forward to. (*sits*) Yes, I've become hard, as you put it. But someone had to. We'd have lost the farm long ago otherwise. I kept us together. No-one else seemed very interested in that when father died.

CHARLOTTE. Why didn't you sell the farm then, when father died? I didn't ask you to keep it. And neither did Millie or Rebecca.

HELENA. You were busy in school. Then went right into nursing. Millie was—Millie was Millie. And Rebecca was a child. Someone had to be strong. Someone had to bring up that child and make sure we'd a certain amount of—(*stops herself*)—No. No-one had to be strong. I was nineteen when father died. And I was young. And I was scared. And this seemed the one thing to hang onto. (MILLIE *and* DENNIS *come bounding in from the past. The lights cross fade.* HELENA *and* CHARLOTTE *exit.*)

SCENE SIX

(*Bright lights come up onstage. We are near the pond.* MILLIE *and* DENNIS HOUSER *enter laughing.* MILLIE *carries a big bowlful of raspberries and an artist's sketchpad.* DENNIS *is the boy on the farm next door; he wears overalls and a checked shirt with an undershirt plainly visible. He has a big smile and lots of hair. They set up for her painting his portrait downcenter.*)

MILLIE. Dennis Houser, how could you speak such an awful lie! Why you make me just *indignant!*

DENNIS. Come on, Millie—don't use words like that.

MILLIE. Well you do! Of course our raspberries are the best in the county.

DENNIS. Are not!

MILLIE. Are so! Now sit down and keep your chin up! (*positions him*)

DENNIS. Maybe I was wrong about the raspberries. Can I try another?

MILLIE. I'm painting "Dennis Houser", not "Dennis Houser Eating Raspberries." Anyway, they're for Charlotte—she's putting up jams. (*He steals one—she slaps his hand.*) Dennis, no! Only way I could get some time off was to promise her this bowlful. (*He takes another and she shoves the bowl in his lap.*) Oh, stuff yourself for all I care!

DENNIS. (*posing*) "Dennis Houser Eating Raspberries!"

MILLIE. (*getting her sketchpad together*) "Dennis Houser making a perfect fool of himself," would be more like it. (*He laughs, obviously pleased that he can irritate her.*) And your eating them, my friend, is just the solid proof! Ours are the best in the county!

DENNIS. Are not!

MILLIE. Then stop eating them!

DENNIS. Okay, it's a tie—the Housers and the Longneckers—first place in the county raspberry contest! (*sits, shaking his leg*)

MILLIE. There's *no* such contest and you know it. Now sit still!

DENNIS. I am sitting still.

MILLIE. Well if that's how you sit still, Dennis Houser, you'd best go take some lessons for all I know. Stop shaking that leg.

DENNIS. You painting my leg?

MILLIE. (*threatening with pencil*) Do you want your portrait done or don't you? (*He stops shaking his leg; she attends to her sketching. Pause, then*)

DENNIS. Well?

MILLIE. Well what?

DENNIS. Well ain't you gonna say anything?

MILLIE. I'm sketching and I can't talk. Much though everyone tells me I'm the smartest of the Longnecker sisters—I cannot do two things at once! You talk— I'll listen!

DENNIS. That's doing two things at once! (*slaps his leg and laughs*) Sketchin' and listenin'—got you there!

MILLIE. Okay, I can do two things. How many can you do? One? A half? Honestly, just sit and talk! Please! (*slight pause*)

DENNIS. Well, I don't know what right to say. I'm Dennis Houser, eldest of the three Houser boys, Mr. Muscle of the Charles T. Brubaker Secondary School.

MILLIE. Mr. Muscle, my eye!

DENNIS. I thought you weren't gonna talk! (*rolls up sleeve*) And I am Mr. Muscle—lookit here! (*presents arm*) Just what do you call that?

MILLIE. I call it an unsightly hairy arm! Sit still.

DENNIS. (*rolls sleeve back*) Oo, Oo, Oo—we're a woman, we've got soft white skin. Can't look at those big hairy men.

MILLIE. I've done my share of looking.

DENNIS. I'll bet you have. (MILLIE *laughs*.) Well, I done my share of lookin' too, Millie. And I sure likes you. I sure gets a kick outta you. Well? (*pause*)

MILLIE. (*sketching*) Well what?

DENNIS. Well ain't you got nothing to say to that? (*She paints*.) Millie?—hey, listen—can I kiss you?

MILLIE. Dennis Houser we're still in secondary school!

DENNIS. Now what's that got to do with anything? My brother's kissed five girls already! And he's younger than me!

MILLIE. Do you mean to tell me Mr. Muscle's never kissed a girl! Oh, wait till that get's around!

DENNIS. Sure I kissed girls.

MILLIE. How many?

DENNIS. Not telling. Aw, come on, Millie—let me kiss you!

MILLIE. Would you tell anybody?

DENNIS. Would you tell anyone you were my first? (MILLIE *puts down her pencil and presents herself to* DENNIS. *He gives her a light peck on the lips*.)

MILLIE. I think, Dennis Houser, there's got to be more in it.

DENNIS. (*frustrated*) I don't got no more to give!

MILLIE. I mean you're supposed to put your hands around me or something. (*He grabs her physically*) Well, don't strangle me!! (*He holds her and gives her a longer, but still innocent kiss. Then he breaks away.*)

DENNIS. Ooooweee! So that's a kiss! Well that sure ain't like kissin' old Aunt Eleanor or huggin' my horse.

MILLIE. (*smooths her dress*) Well I should hope not!

CHARLOTTE. (*offstage*) Millie! Millie Longnecker!— what are you doing down there?

MILLIE. Oh merciful Jesus. (*calls off*) Nothing! Nothing Charlotte!

CHARLOTTE. It sure don't look like nothing. Who's down there with you?

MILLIE. No-one!

CHARLOTTE. Who?

MILLIE.   No-one! It's Dory! Dory!! Dolores Lausch!!!

CHARLOTTE. You be up in half an hour for dinner! And bring Dory with you!

MILLIE. (*to* DENNIS) Now look what you've done.

DENNIS. What-have-I-done? Well—how was I?—can we do it again?

MILLIE. No we cannot! We should get back to this painting.

DENNIS. You liked it didn't you? I knows you did. Hey, Millie, I was your first, too, wasn't I?

MILLIE. I've kissed many a man.

DENNIS. I'll bet.

MILLIE. Well, if I haven't kissed many a man, I'm going to kiss lots of men. Cause my painting's good and I know it! And it's going to take me places! I'm going to kiss Senators and Presidents and Kings and Princes! They'll sit for portraits just like you're sitting there now. And just like you they're going to say: Oh, Millie, Millie please, please kiss me. (*She lays dreamily on her back.*) And I might—and I might not. Depending on my mood. And how handsome they are.

DENNIS. Millie? Am I—well you know—Am I handsome?

MILLIE. Oh, Dennis Houser, eat your raspberries. (REBECCA *enters immediately for the next scene.* DENNIS *and* MILLIE *exit. Lights cross fade to a spot on* REBECCA.)

SCENE SEVEN

(*We are once again in Nebraska.* REBECCA *is pregnant.*)

REBECCA. Helena, my dearest, I write to you personally. And please don't betray my trust by showing this letter to Millie or Charlotte. Things are happening here in Nebraska that I somehow cannot understand. I'm already well into my seventh month—yet honestly, not a single person lifts a hand or finger to aid me now. I still cook, do the laundry, clean up after everyone. It isn't as if I'm the only one working. We're all working, only I've been given all the house chores and everyone else is out in the fields all day. Oh, I don't know—so many times I just want to cry—I must be the loneliest woman west of the Alleghennies. Helena, please, I wish you'd visit me. I don't belong here. I don't know, perhaps I should come East to you. But then—I fear I've already waited too long. (CHARLOTTE *and* HELENA *have already entered for the next scene. They begin talking at once, even before* REBECCA *exits.*)

SCENE EIGHT

(*This scene follows the receipt of* REBECCA's *letter.*
CHARLOTTE *carries her knitting.* HELENA *carries the
just received letter.* CHARLOTTE *sits upleft.* HELENA
stands.)

HELENA. The whole story is utterly sickening.
CHARLOTTE. I can't, I simply can't understand—
HELENA. Understand what!
CHARLOTTE. Why she wouldn't want me to know! Or
Millie.
HELENA. Oh, stop, please! Being insulted is entirely
small and entirely selfish. And will you please put a-
way that knitting. And look at me when I talk to you!
CHARLOTTE. It doesn't distract me.
HELENA. (*furious*) IT DOES ME! (*shoves the letter
in* CHARLOTTE's *lap*) Honestly. We've a girl out there
who's got serious problems! And you choose to sit there
and be childishly insulted. And knit! (CHARLOTTE *puts
down the knitting*) I brought up Rebecca. It's quite
plain why she wrote me.
CHARLOTTE. (*folds her hands in her lap*) I've put
away my knitting.
HELENA. Praise god! (*pause*)
CHARLOTTE. She obviously can't come East. Maybe
you should go out there.
HELENA. I can't go out there. First of all, it'd be
admitting her marriage is an utter failure.
CHARLOTTE. But it is!
HELENA. And that is *not* the point! She's got to find

it in her to understand her husband, to accept his family and like his friends.

CHARLOTTE. Oh, aren't we understanding.

HELENA. Realistic.

CHARLOTTE. And we've such a big heart. Only we choose to give it all to Samuel. (*who this scene is about*)

HELENA. (*slight pause, then*) My relationship with Samuel is my affair, and mine alone. And will not have it subjugated to your simple and frightening puritan zeal. (CHARLOTTE *picks up her knitting and begins to work.*) Anyway, my dear, Samuel's going to California. He's simply stopping in this county, earning some money . . . and visiting his sister.

CHARLOTTE. For six months.

HELENA. He's *visiting* his sister.

CHARLOTTE. Then it's a mighty lengthy visit. (HELENA *slaps her across the face and withdraws quickly.* CHARLOTTE *holds her face*) I'm sorry . . . I—

HELENA. We need a trip, don't we? We need to get away—somewhere, anywhere—just for a while. God, we should take Uncle Jacob's money and go somewhere—West, anywhere, I don't care.

CHARLOTTE. Maybe we should go now—I mean to England.

HELENA. England?

CHARLOTTE. Yes, that's what the money's for. For passage to Manchester. Uncle Jacob still wants us to visit him in Manchester.

HELENA. Why, why would I ever want to go to Manchester? I want to go West. Charlotte, you and Millie and Rebecca—I'm glad I've got you. Believe me, even if I rarely show it.

CHARLOTTE. (*an offer*) Then to Nebraska.

HELENA. (*Suddenly she holds* CHARLOTTE *back at arms length*) What if we sent Rebecca some of the money—Uncle Jacob's money! To buy a farm?

CHARLOTTE. But you can't touch that money.

HELENA. And why not?

CHARLOTTE. Quite simply: I won't allow it. It was given to us—

HELENA. (*moves away from her*) I hardly think it's your option to allow or not to allow—

CHARLOTTE. Uncle Jacob gave us that money for a trip to Manchester. We promised him—

HELENA. What?—What did we promise him? Six years ago we said: Yes, Uncle Jacob, how kind of you, Uncle Jacob.

CHARLOTTE. It was a very generous gift.

HELENA. Oh, please! It was a gift, yes—but to himself! His four sweet nieces would sail across the Atlantic. And present him with family!

CHARLOTTE. He has none! Is that his fault!

HELENA. Is it mine? Honestly, what a waste. Sitting there collecting interest for six years.

CHARLOTTE. Where it will sit—six more years if need be. Until we go to Manchester.

HELENA. Must you follow every single promise? Every little rule?

CHARLOTTE. Yes! You think me slow and over-religious and god fearing. You find fault in every part of me I happen to cling to and respect. I judge human nature poorly. I'm a little puritan.

HELENA. I never said—

CHARLOTTE. What else! What else do you want to hit me with? What else? Well, you won't touch that money. Go! Go West with Samuel! Make love to him over every inch of land from here to the Pacific. Take him and enjoy him! But you won't touch that money! Not a cent! (*She rushes out. There is a slow hold on Helena and then* MILLIE *and* UNCLE JACOB *are heard laughing offstage;* HELENA *remains in place for the following scene.*)

SCENE NINE

(*The stage is completely bare and we are at the cemetery. A flood of bright light covers the stage, giving
us the sense of a cool and crisp Spring day. Downleft
will be the tombstone of Ezekial Turner, downright
will be the tombstones of Mr. and Mrs. Longnecker—
all three imagined. From upleft enter* MILLIE *and*
UNCLE JACOB, *walking arm in arm. Behind them are*
CHARLOTTE *and* REBECCA. *The women may be wear-
ing lacy shawls;* MILLIE *may even have placed some
flowers in her hair;* HELENA *and* CHARLOTTE *may
have two frilly sun parasols—everything to give this
the impression of a Sunday outing.* UNCLE JACOB
*wears spectacles, is vested and physically overbear-
ing. He is astute, practical, pragmatic and insecure.
His need for the love of his nieces is large—as is
his inability to truly understand them or know how
to love them.*)

MILLIE. (*as they enter*) I come here quite often,
Uncle Jacob. Well, not quite so often. But I do like
to come up here and sketch the tombstones and think
about all these names.

UNCLE JACOB. A pretty face like your's? Helena,
what've you done to this girl?

HELENA. She's turned out maudlin. By choice, not by
influence.

MILLIE. I'm not maudlin! And I'm not a pretty face
or a girl either, Uncle Jacob. I'm seventeen! And next
year I'm going to Philadelphia to study art. By myself!

CHARLOTTE. We'll see about that.

REBECCA. I don't know why anybody'd want to go to stupid old Philadelphia.

MILLIE. Oh, Rebecca, what do you know?

REBECCA. Lots. I'm in secondary school, too, you know. (UNCLE JACOB *is just delighted by this sort of chatter.*)

HELENA. (*smiling*) One doesn't know "lots." One knows "a lot." (REBECCA *rolls her eyes.*)

MILLIE. (*crossing left, pulls him with her*) But, Uncle Jacob, I don't think about death. I think about the lives of all these people. Look here! Here's one of my favorites! Zekial Turner! Isn't that a marvelous name! (*draws it out*) Ezekial Turner!

UNCLE JACOB. (*reading off the tomb*) Born 1676. Died 1722.

MILLIE. Imagine being born in the 1600's. And he lived to see a new century—like we will!

UNCLE JACOB. Probably killed by your Indians.

MILLIE. Now that's maudlin! I've always thought he died in his sleep. Just lying there restful, you know, giving up his soul like a flower cut by frost. (*wrapped up in her thoughts*) That's how I want to go.

REBECCA. Are we all going to die, Uncle Jacob? I mean like momma and poppa? Are we just gonna lie there in the ground?

UNCLE JACOB. Yes. I'm afraid so, my child. That's why we've got to give each other a bit of ourselves before we go.

REBECCA. I don't think I was left a bit of momma. I don't remember momma. Not at all.

HELENA. (*moves to* REBECCA) Rebecca, I'll take you back to the carriage.

REBECCA. No, I'm all right. I keep trying to remember her. But I just keep getting all these faces confused. I keep on seeing you or Charlotte. (CHARLOTTE *moves to* REBECCA.)

CHARLOTTE. She remembers you. She's looking down at you all the time—thinking of you, hoping you'll turn out to be the woman she wanted you to be.

REBECCA. I don't ever want to be a woman.

CHARLOTTE. But she wants you to be. (REBECCA *takes a few steps to the imagined graves.*)

REBECCA. I'll make you so proud, momma. I'm going to have children and make you so proud. You watch me, momma. You watch just how much I make with my life. Yes, momma,—I'm going to be a woman just like you. (*She returns back to* CHARLOTTE *who embraces her.* UNCLE JACOB *moves over to* REBECCA, *kisses her, and then moves to confront his brother's grave, making a long cross from downleft to downright.*)

UNCLE JACOB. (*Slowly takes off his spectacles and puts them away*) Peter Longnecker. 1838 to 1888. Lived half a century. Exactly. Is that all there is? A name, two dates. A wife beside you with her name and her dates too? Peter, I've a fine industry now. Textiles. Eighty-three employees back in Manchester, working on my looms. Wish to damn you might have come and seen me. Wish to damn I could have seen you. Never got married, Peter. No, never married. (HELENA *turns to face upstage, unquieted.*) I'm sorry—you must believe me—sorry there was an ocean between us. (*turns to face the girls*) He got sick of Europe. Strong-headed. Guess you know that.

HELENA. My god! I had so much. My god, so much of me, so much of me is lost. (*her voice cracks*)

CHARLOTTE. (*immediately to* MILLIE) Take Rebecca to the carriage. (MILLIE *and* REBECCA *exit hesitantly.*) Helena, they loved us. Very much. You know that.

HELENA. I don't want this life. I don't want any part of my worthless, worthless life.

CHARLOTTE. Of course you do.

HELENA. (*breaks from* CHARLOTTE) NO! You don't understand! I stood there looking at those graves. I wanted love—anything!—to take hold of me. But my god, Charlotte, all I could feel was—How could you die on me!! My life! *My dreams!* How could you, both of you, die on me? (*collapsing into* CHARLOTTE's *arms*) Oh, Charlotte.

UNCLE JACOB. (*pause, then*) I'm sorry. I never knew. (*another pause, he removes a small bankbook from his pocket*) Here. I've got something for you. At the bank yesterday ... I put some money in. Enough for a passage to Manchester. That's what it's for. For passage to Manchester. For each of you. So you can all come over and visit me. Stay as long as you please —a month, a year. Americans are very popular in Europe right now. Especially wealthy ones.

CHARLOTTE. Thank you. Thank you, Uncle Jacob.

UNCLE JACOB. Here. (*gives it to* CHARLOTTE) Now you book yourselves passage with haste. I think my nieces need a fine vacation. I'll show you off to all of Manchester. Now you promise to come?

CHARLOTTE. We do. We promise. Sometime soon. (*starts to exit with her uncle.*)

UNCLE JACOB. Now we better be getting back to the carriage. Or else Rebecca and Millie will think we enjoy standing about in cemeteries. Why don't you wait until next Spring, till the weather clears up. Manchester's so full of flowers in the Spring. We'll have such a fine time, the five of us! Such a fine time when you come! (*He exists with* CHARLOTTE. HELENA *is joined by* SAMUEL *for the following scene. Lights cross fade.*)

SCENE TEN

(*The lights go up very bright and very white. It is summer—one of those late June days in Pennsylvania when the sudden heat and humidity take you by surprise, marking the sure end of Spring. We are at the raspberry patch, imagined.* HELENA *stands downright; she has a flirtatious and expectant look on her face; she's opened her blouse a bit and has a handkerchief in her sleeve—during the scene she'll dab her forehead and neck with it. The bushes run downstage along the apron.* SAMUEL *stands a few feet back, center stage, where he has placed a wooden bucket with a ladle in it. He has unbottoned his collar a bit, and also has a handkerchief to wipe his face. Though they've known each other for weeks, this is a first date.*)

SAMUEL. (*He holds a rather large black ledger; they are going over the farm's receipts.*) And we spent seven dollars on new planking for the barn. The fence on the north acres needs some more wire. I ordered it, but until it comes, I've asked the men not to use it.

HELENA. (*not terribly concerned*) Did you pay them?

SAMUEL. Gave Jake and Scottie twenty extra. For the work they did last April. Think I should've given them more?

HELENA. (*dabs her neck and smiles*) Did you have it? (*turns her back to him, facing the audience. She opens her collar flirtatiously*)

SAMUEL. No. Not really. But they're good boys, and this way they won't mind some extra work. Scottie's getting married, you know. And we went through the supplies last week.

HELENA. (*laughs*) You always say "we."

SAMUEL. I beg your pardon.

HELENA. You always say "we." We did this. We did that. Isn't there just one of you?

SAMUEL. It's just an expression. Do you want me to go on with this? (*She smiles and shakes her head.*)

HELENA. Scottie's getting married. Does that mean we'll have to look for someone else then?

SAMUEL. Oh, I think he's happy.

HELENA. And yourself?

SAMUEL. Oh I'm very happy.

HELENA. No, I mean California. I just want to be —well, you know—*prepared* for when you leave. Do you know?

SAMUEL. (*he plays with her*) Well . . . *we* looked at *our* savings last week—

HELENA. (*mock admonition*) You. Singular, Samuel. *You* looked at *your* savings last week.

SAMUEL. (*They both smile.*) It's the heat.

HELENA. I know. June twenty-first, the first day of summer, and just look at these raspberries. Already rotting on the vine. If this is June, good god I don't want to even think about July. Or August.

SAMUEL. (*who has moved to get a drink of water from the bucket*) Sun should go down in a few minutes. Then it should cool off some. Water?

HELENA. (*turns her back to him again*) I'll go up to the house soon and make some tea. (SAMUEL *looks at her back, then decides to take off his shirt, and does so while she's talking.*) My father planted these raspberries. I've always been surprised that something so good can come from so little labor. So. You didn't answer me. (*stoops*) If you're going to California, I'd just like to know (*stands up*)—when you think you'll be (*turns to face him*) leaving. Oh.

SAMUEL. You don't mind, do you? (*turns to pick up the ledger from the ground—she doesn't take her eyes off him*) Listen. Maybe we should just go back to the ledger.

HELENA. (*turning away*) May I say something? I mean would you be awfully insulted if—

SAMUEL. Helena, no, please, go right ahead.

HELENA. I know everyone's moving west. There's this great wave across the continent right now. But surely you're a little bit more objective. Surely you can't believe San Francisco's paved with gold, no matter what they say. You understand, do as you please. I just don't want you to go off to California. And then be surprised.

SAMUEL. I won't be.

HELENA. That's all I wanted.

SAMUEL. And I'm not going to California to be rich.

HELENA. (*realizing things got a bit testy*) Really. This is most unfortunate. I only meant—

SAMUEL. Haven't you ever thought to go west, Helena? Just to forget about the farm, wave goodbye to your sisters ... And head out west past the Rockies?

HELENA. Well, I imagine, at one time or another ... But you must understand, Samuel. I've obligations. And responsibilities.

SAMUEL. Well so have I. But to myself. I count myself first.

HELENA. That's where we—(*catches her frank tone, but not in time to change it*)—differ then. Really. I shouldn't have asked you down here. We could've gone over the ledger up in the house. Where it's cooler.

SAMUEL. Haven't you ever looked over that hill where the sun's setting right now? Haven't you ever thought life's just got to be, it just has to be better than *what is?* I'm going to California, Helena, because I'm awful tired of the East Coast. I'm tired of the milkman and the doctor and the paper everyday. Everyone's alway coming at you, telling you what to do, what to think. Well, I've had enough. And as soon as I've saved up enough money, I'm getting out. And if you'd any sense about you, you'd want to get out also. You'd kiss Millie and Charlotte goodbye, sell this place, And—(*stops himself*)

HELENA. And what?

SAMUEL. And nothing.

HELENA. But you must have meant something?

SAMUEL. You sit here—I've seen you—on the back porch—late at night. You want something. When are you going to say: Me. It's my chance. What I want. Me! (*offers her water*)

HELENA. (*moves to take it from him; he moves away*) I said that once. I did. But it was a very long time ago. And no-one listened anyway.

SAMUEL. Why didn't you sell the farm when your father died? (HELENA *makes a motion with her hand, as if to say something, but doesn't*) I'm sorry.

HELENA. (*Still caught up in this, she moves down-left*) There's no need to be sorry.

SAMUEL. You don't have to answer. I mean you don't even have to answer yourself. Oh—there it goes!—Just a thin slip of red left . . . there, on the bottom of the sky. (*She faces him.*) And now! . . . (*moves to downright*) And now!—gone. Forever. All the light of June twenty-first, the first day of summer, eighteen ninety four: gone forever. And we'll never see it again. (*pause*) Listen. You can just begin to hear the crickets.

HELENA. (*after a moment*) There are some things in life, Samuel, that are so private. Things that should . . . shouldn't be said to just anyone. After mother died and father was so sick—I was very young: very young and very pretty and very smart. My goodness, Spring slides into your life. And suddenly you're a young wo-men instead of a girl. Suddenly the idea of sharing your life with someone: that doesn't seem like such a silly notion anymore. There was one young man in particular: Jason Armstrong. The son of Mr. Armstrong of the bank in town. I think you know him. (*repeats the name to herself, smiling*) Jason Armstrong. It was the summer right after my commencement. Everyday had a breeze and—my god, there are times in life when everything's so perfect. Everyday you wake up to sun on your lace curtains—And the whole house smells of lilacs. You want to hang onto it, clutch it, bag it up for those not so perfect days that lie ahead. We spent much of that summer together, Jason and I. Yet father was so sick. Spitting up blood. Passing water on his bedsheets so I had to change them everyday. When August came, I said to myself: god, father dies and this family's going to fall apart like pick up sticks. However. Jason had just finished college and was going to New York to work for his uncle. One day, in late August, a day like today when the heat really did come upon us, I said to Jason: Please! Take me away. I don't want to live here anymore. Please, marry me! And that was it . . . Jason said I didn't love him—all I really wanted was escape. And that was it . . . Like some train stopped and I was asked to disembark at this station. Where I still am. Where I've prooved with utter vengeance how very little I wanted escape. And am as you find me today: Sitting on the back porch. Pulling stems off blades of grass. (*They look at one another a moment*) Really. I should've kept this to the ledger.

SAMUEL. Come with me.

HELENA. What?

SAMUEL. I said come with me. To California. With me. (*moves to her*)

HELENA. I can't.

SAMUEL. Yes you can, Helena. It's not—

HELENA. No, Samuel, I can't. It's unthinkable. (*She turns to go, he grabs her hand and forces her to face him.*)

SAMUEL. Helena, I've been looking at you. Night after night. Seeing that you want—

HELENA. Samuel, please, let go of me!

SAMUEL. You've been here all these years. Waiting for something. Looking out, asking for so much to come to you.

HELENA. Samuel, please!

SAMUEL. Wanting so much. Desiring so much. (*She struggles a moment to be free. He pulls her towards him and kisses her with strength. The scene fades. Music announcing another scene in the present. As the lights cross fade,* SAMUEL *exits, and* HELENA *is joined by her sisters.*)

SCENE ELEVEN

(*The present once again.* HELENA *and* CHARLOTTE *are seated.* MILLIE *and* REBECCA *enter from upright,* MILLIE *holding her sketchpad and several pencils.*)

MILLIE. (*as they enter*) Now, Rebecca, I want you to sit down, keep your chin up—and don't move a muscle. (*as she positions* REBECCA) You really are very pretty. Look at your skin: milky, not a blemish. I'd give a lot, Rebecca, to have skin like yours.

HELENA. You're very pretty, Millie.

MILLIE. I wasn't fishing. Just commenting. There, Rebecca, don't move an inch. (MILLIE *sits.*)

REBECCA. My eyes. I've always had the brightest eyes. I remember momma kissing my eyes and telling me they were like beacons. Like beacons to my soul.

Seems to me they'd be a lot more useful if they were beacons to someone else's soul.

MILLIE. (*aftter she absorbs this*) Rebecca, I hate to admit it, but you are the prettiest. No, I don't even hate to admit it. I remember our teachers comparing us. Helena was the most articulate, the most forceful. Charlottte was always the little lady. Not unkind, Charlotte. I was the smartest though I'm not sure how smart, or if any of that intelligence ever finally paid off. And, Rebecca, here in front of me. Skin so pure. Eyes, like mother said, either looking out. Searching. Or warning of something much darker. Some hazard. (*pause*) Oh, I never wanted to be an artist. All I wanted was the fame.

MR. KARONK. (*offstage, a loud boisterous voice*) Helloah! Helloah! Anybody home? Is anybody in here?

HELENA. Oh, thank god. In here, Mr. Karonk! Millie, Charlotte. (*She rises.*)

MR. KARONK. (*still off*) Is anybody home? This is such a big—

HELENA. (*forceful*) In here Mr. Karonk!!

MR. KARONK. (*enters, a big busy-body handiman*) Ah! So here we are! You've got a lot of rooms out there. One could get lost.

HELENA. But you didn't. Mr. Karonk, I'm Helena—

MR. KARONK. That's Karonk. K-A-R-O-N-K! Dutch! (*correcting her pronunciation, which has been wrong since* MILLIE *first said his name*)

HELENA. I'm terribly sorry.

MR. KARONK. Don't be. Just get it right. Earl Karonk. Of Karonk's Shipping and Handling. Twelve Chestnut Street, Philadelphia. (*with bravura*) My card. (*gives one to each*) I just had these printed up. Two ink colors, can you imagine. What's the world coming to?

HELENA. That's very nice, Mr. Karonk.

MR. KARONK. Karonk! K-A-R-O-N-K! My great great grandfather emigrated from Kurkie. Dutch East Indies Company. Ever heard of it?

HELENA. Charlotte, Millie—are we ready?

MR. KARONK. Ready for what? Ladies, ladies, we've got a problem. We've got a problem and we're not going anywhere.

CHARLOTTE. Helena.

MR. KARONK. And I saw that problem on the front porch right when I came in. In a word, ladies: the bags! Too many, and too heavy!

CHARLOTTE. The bags?—Mr. Karonk—

MR. KARONK. That's Karonk!!

CHARLOTTE. We've but a few bags.

MR. KARONK. But a few bags? BUT A FEW BAGS?? There are thirteen bags out there, ladies! And they're not bags! They're trunks!! Big ones!! Heavy ones!! (*controls himself, sits*) So. I'm going to need assistance. A volunteer. Raise your hand up, the one of you —up, up, up. Which one's it going to be?

MILLIE. This is ridiculous.

MR. KARONK. It's preposterous. That's exactly what it is.

CHARLOTTE. My dear man! The neighboring farm. It's the Houser's. Dennis Houser. He'd be only too glad to help.

MILLIE. Charlotte!!

MR. KARONK. What's the name? Houser?

CHARLOTTE. Out the back door, then right down the path. You can't miss it. (*He exits, mumbling.*) Honestly. Why didn't he bring someone.

HELENA. Rebecca, dear, sit down again. Millie hasn't finished her sketch of you.

MILLIE. Rebecca. Look at me, dear. Have any of us had children.

HELENA. Millie! How could you?

MILLIE. Have we?

MILLIE. Well, how could Charlotte do that? Just tell him to go get Dennis! I don't want to see Dennis again. Not now! Not ever! (MILLIE *instantly calls out Dennis' name, and the lights cross fade sharply to an evening exterior. Her sisters exit.*)

SCENE TWELVE

(*Moonlit night near the pond.*)

MILLIE. (*calling off*) Dennis! Deeennnissss! Hurry up! Or the moon'll go down and we won't see a thing. (*She grabs a blanket and hamper that have been preset upstage, below a ramp. Then she moves downright center to set up for her evening with* DEN-NIS. *She throws open the quilt or blanket and smooths it out.*) Dennis! You move much slower and you'll have to give up your manhood—and become a snail. (*opens the hamper and takes out a small jug of whiskey*) Or fish! I saw fish jumping in the pond, Dennis. (DENNIS *enters from upstage; he is overladen with pillows.* MIL-LIE *hasn't seen him and moves downstage with her drink. He plops the stuff down and quietly creeps up on her.*) Dennis Houser, I propose a toast. To the moonlight on the pond—cause that's god's work. To Millie Longnecker for having finished art school. And to you, Dennis Houser, on your twenty-first birthday! (*She drinks and Dennis slaps her on her rear.*)

DENNIS. Caught you drinking on the sideline.

MILLIE. Oh, you beast! Don't you ever do that again.

DENNIS. And why not?

MILLIE. Cause I'm a woman. That's why not!

DENNIS. I slaps Roberta there all the time.

MILLIE. Dennis Houser, I'm a *woman. Roberta's* a horse.

DENNIS. (*picking up bottle*) Some woman—drinking sour-mash whiskey.

MILLIE. It sooths me. It comforts my weary soul.

DENNIS. (*childlike sarcasm*) Ooooo—we're an artist. We've such a weary soul.

MILLIE. You idiot! Twenty-one! Twenty-one and you've yet to grow up.

DENNIS. That's right! And I'm gonna start growing down. I don't like being twenty-one.

MILLIE. But how do *you* know? You haven't been twenty-one a day yet! (*goes to the hamper*) Oh, oh, oh, oh. You're not going to raise my temper tonight, Dennis Houser. (*digs into hamper*) No sir, no sir. It's your birthday, the moon's like a beacon and (*takes package out and hands it to him*) I'm not going to be riled by you. Here.

DENNIS. What is it?

MILLIE. A present, stupid. A *birth*day present. Open it.

DENNIS. I mean—well—what is it?

MILLIE. It's a present—I can't tell you what it is. Open it and find out.

DENNIS. (*puts it behind him*) I'll wait till tomorrow.

MILLIE. Tomorrow? Tomorrow's not your birthday! For crying out loud, Dennis: OPEN IT! (*He opens it.*) It was on special. So you have to like it. I mean I can't return it. I mean I didn't have much money. I mean—well, do you like it?

DENNIS. (*pulls out pipe, sticks it in his mouth and poses*) Dennis Houser smoking pipe!

MILLIE. (*takes it from his mouth*) Dennis Houser making a perfect fool of himself.

DENNIS. (*takes it back*) Aw, come on, Millie. I love it. I'll smoke it every day.

MILLIE. (*taking box*) And there's some tobacco. And special matches. Well. Aren't you going to light it?

DENNIS. Now?

MILLIE. Of course now! I want to see how it works.

DENNIS. It's a pipe. That's how it works.

MILLIE. But I've never smoked a pipe before.

DENNIS. You? You mean you wanna smoke it?

MILLIE. Of course I do! (*hands box back to him. Then she props up some pillows on the blanket, drinks and lies down. He stuffs the pipe and then lies beside her.*) I bought it in Philly and the man just about fell over on seeing a woman in his tobacco shop. But I acted like it was all quite normal. Like I buy pipes for all my menfolk. Anyway, I was carrying my sketchboard and he probably thought: Well, this one's a looney. *Quelle artiste!*

DENNIS. (*lights pipe*) All your menfolk—what's that mean?

MILLIE. I wrote you. I was proposed to twice. By an attorney. And a dentist. Oh, the types one meets in Philadelphia. Can you imagine?—I mean marrying a dentist. Yeuch! (*She drinks and then passes him the bottle.*) To you.

DENNIS. To me. (*He drinks.*) Seems to me a dentist could give you a real fine life.

MILLIE. I've no intention of leading a real fine life. You know that. I mean can you imagine—with his hands in people's mouth all the time. Good lord!

DENNIS. Millie, I wanna tell you something.

MILLIE. And I want to smoke that pipe.

DENNIS. Can't you wait! Just a second. I got something on my mind and I wanna speak it. I wanna thank you, Millie. I mean for keeping me on as your friend.

MILLIE. Dennis.

DENNIS. Now wait a minute! I mean you went off to art school. And I stayed back here and worked dad's farm. I never been to college. And I don't see any of that in my future at all. I mean my education's limited.

MILLIE. (*sitting up*) But you're not.

DENNIS. Will you let me talk! Please! Just like a woman—always interrupting! (MILLIE *plops back down.*) What I mean to say is—well, you've been good to me. I seen a little bit of the world from your eyes. I mean, shucks. I ain't never gonna get to *Philadelphia.* That aint me. But I mean you talk to me, you tell me about your school, the artists, the music you hear, the (*mispronounces*) theater.

MILLIE. (*corrects him*) Theater.

DENNIS. Theater. Well, I don't know how to say this. But that ain't my life out there. I don't read *books.* I don't got no time for *books.* When I gots a minute free—well, all I wants to do is laugh or drink or come on down to the pond here when you're back. What I'm trying to say is—well, it's good to know all that's going on out there. I mean I never would have known it if I hadn't known you. And don't get me wrong—it don't help me none when I got thirty acres to plow. It don't ease the hurt I feel when I got up at four and don't get to bed till way past dark. But, well, it's kindda reassuring. And I thanks you.

MILLIE. Now can I smoke the pipe.

DENNIS. You didn't hear a word I said!

MILLIE. I did! You're reassured.

DENNIS. (*turns away*) Oh, it's no use talking to you. All you wanna hear's your own voice.

MILLIE. Dennis. Come on, Dennis. (*mildly childish*)

Mr. Muscle. Dennis Houser posing as a log. (*He turns to face her smiling.*) I'm glad. (*kisses him lightly*) Glad you told me that. (*He hands her the pipe, she poses.*) Millie Longnecker as a big old fat Southern planter. (*She takes a puff and chokes.*)

DENNIS. You silly! Don't inhale it!! (*She tries again, this time successfully. They both lie back again, and, through the following scene, hand the pipe back and forth.*)

MILLIE. And now I want to tell you something. (*throughout following lines,* MILLIE *puts the jug, tobacco, matches and pipe back in the hamper.*)

DENNIS. I promise not to interrupt. Cause I'm a man.

MILLIE. Oh, I won't be long. I just want to thank you too. You've been here. Someone I can talk to. You're solid—you know what I mean? I mean let's say you're confused—but your confusion's a real solid sort of confusion. And mine's not. Mine's very frail. But I know I can come back here to you. Off I go making myself into a *quelle artiste,* drinking whiskey, smoking pipes. And yet none of that really disturbs you. I can come back here, and lay beside you. And tell you what's whizzing through my mind.

DENNIS. Good old Dennis. The stick in the mud.

MILLIE. (*jabs him with her elbow*) You're not a stick in the mud. And you're not old! Anyhow, in my own way—now don't get upset—but I know I love you. That doesn't upset you, does it?

DENNIS. (*smoking pipe*) No, no.

MILLIE. And though you'll never admit it in a thousand years, I know you love me too. (*pause*)

DENNIS. Millie?

MILLIE. It's so silent out. You can hear the fish jumping.

DENNIS. Millie, you ain't waiting for me, are you?

MILLIE. (*faces him*) Don't you want to hear the fish jumping?

DENNIS. I mean you ain't waiting for me to propose. (*She stares at him.*) Cause I ain't never gonna. Our lives're like this—right side by side. Like our farms are. And yet we're miles and years away from one another.

MILLIE. (*her voice cracks*) The fish—are jumping.

DENNIS. Millie. Please don't cry on me.

MILLIE. (*shaking, trying to hold it all back*) I can't help it. I can't help it. (*She cries—he holds her.*)

DENNIS. You ain't never thought I'd propose, now, did you? I mean you're so much *smarter* than me. You never couldda thought that. I mean I've got my own life to lead! I'm twenty-one! I gots to get started on something. And quick.

MILLIE. No, I always knew we'd never marry.

DENNIS. (*stands up*) Millie? I'm courting somebody. But you knows her and I won't tell you her name.

MILLIE. (*she stands*) You can tell me.

DENNIS. Dolores Lausch.

MILLIE. Dorry Lausch!

DENNIS. Now don't you go cutting her down! (MILLIE *turns away.*) I know she isn't you! But I couldn't marry a woman like you! And I'm courting *her*. And in a few months I might just pop the question. Millie? Millie? And I wants to be able to thank you for something else! Thank you cause you're gonna wish me good luck.

MILLIE. Dorry Lausch?

DENNIS. Millie!!

MILLIE. (*goes to him and kisses him lightly*) You have it then. (*holds his head in her hands*) Oh, my Dennis Houser, my Dennis Houser. I give you all the luck I've got in the world.

DENNIS. (*holds her*) You ain't hurt?

MILLIE. Unprepared. Let's leave it at that. Look— the moon's gone down. (*breaks away*) I've got the most brilliant idea. Let's go swimming!

DENNIS. But I ain't got my outfit!

MILLIE. (*starts to undress*) So what?

DENNIS. So what? Millie! Stop that right now!

MILLIE. You can just sit here for all I care. Be a little coward.

DENNIS. (*starts to take off his shirt*) Well, I'm no coward! I'm just as good as the rest of them! (*stops*) But Millie—Millie—I mean— well, you'll see me!

MILLIE. No I won't. I said the moon's gone down. Anyway, Dennis Houser, this is 1893. And that's not the Middle Ages! (*He starts to undress and the lights cross fade for scene thirteen. MILLIE runs off, carrying the hamper. REBECCA and UNCLE JACOB enter and sit downleft and upright respectively. Center stage darkens. HELENA enters and joins the man there.*)

SCENE THIRTEEN

(REBECCA *and* UNCLE JACOB *are isolated in two pools of light. They each carry the handwork they refer to.* UNCLE JACOB *is dictating.*)

UNCLE JACOB. My four most dear nieces across the Atlantic. No, no—scratch that. My Helena, Charlotte, Mi—no, no. I can't begin this thing. My four ... my four dearest nieces in America. Yes, write that! My four dearest nieces et cetera. I fear this may be my last letter to you. (*to his secretary*) Don't look at me. Keep your eye on that page.

REBECCA. Just a quick note to you, Helena, my dearest, my ever so dear sister. First, I was a little surprised. I thought surely you'd come visit me. But second—the money for the farm!—oh, Helena, I thank you and my soon to arrive child thanks you for the money.

UNCLE JACOB. I'm quite ill. And the doctors here can't seem to tell me what it is. Their ignorance as to the disease assures me death is imminent. And that I should now tie together the loose ends of my life. Quite funny—eh?—coming from a textile manufacturer. (*looks up*) No, no! Don't write that down, you stupid! That was to you. And now don't waste time erasing it either!

REBECCA. This may be silly, but I daren't let anyone know I've got the money. As they'd be sure to grab it and put it on this worthless hole of a place. Helena, you've given me my freedom. And my baby freedom! I've taken to sewing for the baby—diapers and smocks.

UNCLE JACOB. The doctors have requested that I take up knitting or crocheting. Remarkable. As to the loose ends. I am bequeathing you my home, my lands, my industry and each and every of my worldly possessions. The amount I leave is considerable, if not overwhleming. For this reason, I have drawn up my will in such manner, that if you decide not to opt for England . . . the entirety shall be sold and the money given to charity. Which should make some orphans overjoyed.

REBECCA. I hope it's a girl and I can name her after momma or you. Peter wants a son, but that's just because a boy might be more useful on a farm—though we got along very well, didn't we! Oh, I'm going to give my child all the best in the world! She's going to eat raspberries and cream all the days of her life! And she'll be even prettier than I am.

UNCLE JACOB. You've the money from six years ago. That shall be for passage here to Manchester. I'm sorry—sorry you never came. But that is the extent of my feeling. Sorrow—not resentment. You could have quite a time here—young, wealthy American women. I'm just sorry that I won't be able to see— But perhaps the British orphans will praise you. Is that it? Amelia? —how is your painting? And Rebecca?—your marriage? Am I a great uncle now? Charlotte, will you pray for me? As if we were all living in the country some time ago . . . and there was no industry . . . and no money! . . . and we all depended on the land for sustenance!

REBECCA. I'll write you when I've delivered. And maybe you can come and see my new baby! And my new farm!

UNCLE JACOB. I've more things to say. Helena. More things. Passing. My deepest love.

REBECCA. Just think of it!

UNCLE JACOB. Post that! (*Cross fade to center stage revealing* HELENA *and* SAMUEL *asleep. As* SAMUEL *starts to talk,* REBECCA *and* UNCLE JACOB *exit.*)

SCENE FOURTEEN

(*The lights rise on* HELENA *and* SAMUEL. *They lie on a huge stage pillow and are covered with a large brown blanket. Their clothes lay strewn to the left of them. It is night, midsummer.*)

SAMUEL. (*after a moment*) Helena? (*no response; he sits up, yawns*) Helena. Helena, my leg's cramped. (*He moves it, she rolls over on her back. He takes his leg out from under the blanket and rubs it.*) Aren't you glad it's summer.

HELENA. Hmmmm.

SAMUEL. I said: aren't you glad it's summer. (*pokes her*) Helena?

HELENA. (*half seductively*) You always begin everything, "I said."

SAMUEL. That's because you don't listen the first time.

HELENA. That isn't true. Why should I be glad it's summer? (*kisses him*)

SAMUEL. If it weren't summer, where'd we go every night? I mean we can't go to my sister's. Not to mention your sisters'.

HELENA. Get some clothes on. Honestly.

SAMUEL. That's just what I meant about summer. Outside—no clothes—it doesn't matter. But what are we going to do come Winter? Have you ever thought—

HELENA. (*cuts him off*) Quite simply—we'll go inside. Will you please get dressed.

SAMUEL. Who's going to see us down here? God?— he doesn't care. Charlotte?—oh . . . that would be funny.

HELENA. Charlotte knows about us.

SAMUEL. She what?

HELENA. I *said*: Charlotte knows about us. Samuel, I had to tell her. What if someone came over to the house at night. Then Charlotte could make up some legitimate excuse for my absence. And yours! Now will you please put some clothes on!

SAMUEL. The only legitimate excuse is I love you. (*kisses her passionately then leans over to grab his shirt*) Now just you wait a minute, Miss Helena Longnecker. I've got something for you. I ordered them special as you can't pick these up at any old station. Ah, here we are. (*presents an envelope to her*)

HELENA. (*opening it*) I can't imagine—(*pulls out two tickets*)—what are they?

SAMUEL. Two tickets! To California by train.

HELENA. (*joyously*) California?

SAMUEL. But they're special tickets. I mean they're good for a whole year. We don't have to state the time yet.

HELENA. (*laughs*) But my man, my sweet man— where, where does this come from?

SAMUEL. (*pointing*) B and O Railroad. Main office.

HELENA. No, no, I mean, Samuel, you haven't proposed yet.

SAMUEL. And I'm not going to.

HELENA. Well then you can just take these right back.

SAMUEL. You don't understand! Not now, Helena! But the minute we cross that glorious border—from Nevada to California!—I'm going to take you in my arms and say: Helena, Miss Longnecker, will you please be my wife?

HELENA. (*throws herself at him*) Yes, yes!

SAMUEL. NOT NOW! I don't want to get married here. We'd settle down. We'd have kids or something. And then just how in hell would we ever get to California? Helena, please!

HELENA. But children have made the crossing before.

SAMUEL. But *ours* are going to be *born* in California. They're going to know the East Coast second hand. Cause second hand's the only way to know the East Coast. Oh, Helena, please!

HELENA. But my sisters—

SAMUEL. They can throw you a shower. But I'm making it clear. No wedding. Not now. We'll board the train and start out West. And we can even stop in Nebraska and see your sister. And her child if it's born yet! But then we're back onboard! Across the plains! Across the Rockies! And at the very first signpost of California!—

HELENA. Yes! Yes, I accept!

SAMUEL. (*grabbing her*) I knew you would! I knew you would! I knew you would!! (*They kiss. Lights cross fade to a downtown exterior.* MILLIE *and* CHARLOTTE *enter laughing; they have been window shopping.* HELENA *and* SAMUEL *grab their clothes, the blanket and pillow and exit.*)

SCENE FIFTEEN

(*We are downtown. Stage lights up full.*)

MILLIE. And when I went to pick up the cotton for Rebecca—(*laughs*) Well, I asked Mr. Bombeck if he remembered how long I'd had it on order. Oh, the men in this town, either pompous and dry, or ugly and dry. Philadelphia men are so much more—

CHARLOTTE. (*calls out to an imagined passerby*) Good morning, Mr. Murphy.

MILLIE. Oh, good morning, Mr. Murphy.

CHARLOTTE. (*to* MR. MURPHY) Yes, it's very sad about Uncle Jacob.

MILLIE. Well, he said to me in his deep burly voice: No, madame. And then I said to him: I thought I was still a madamoiselle—Where's the husband? Where's the husband? And he didn't know what I meant. (*to another passerby*) Morning, Mrs. Chester.

CHARLOTTE. Good morning, Mrs. Chester. Mr. Bombeck! "Mr. Bombast" it should be. Did he keep scratching at his nose?

MILLIE. Precisely. And picking at his ear. (*They laugh and are greeted by two passerbys.*) Good morning Dr. Zeigler, Mrs. Zeigler.

CHARLOTTE. Morning, Dr. Zeigler, Mrs. Zeigler. (*stops for a moment*)

MILLIE. Are you all right, Charlotte?

CHARLOTTE. (*quickly*) Of course I am.

MILLIE. (*to another passerby*) Dolores Lausch!!

CHARLOTTE. Morning, Dorry Lausch!

MILLIE. And good morning to you! (*all smiles, but through her teeth*) She still has the ugliest hair I've ever seen.

CHARLOTTE. Shh!—she'll hear you.

MILLIE. Well she does! (*They start to exit.*) Dorry Lausch— honestly, the way people dress around here. Charlotte, believe me, no-one in Philadelphia would be caught dead with hair like that! (*And they are gone. Music announcing another scene in the present, as the sisters enter.*)

SCENE SIXTEEN

(*We are in the present once again. The sisters sit in silence a moment, MILLIE sketching REBECCA. Immediately, DENNIS and MR. KARONK are heard approaching.*)

MR. KARONK. Well, ladies, look who the cat dragged in! (*He laughs heartily.*)

DENNIS. I was on my way over anyway.

MR. KARONK. I understand Mr. Houser here has bought this place. Isn't that right, Mr. Houser.

DENNIS. Dennis, sir. You can call me Dennis.

MR. KARONK. Would you mind?—I'm just really curious—business interests you see—but how much did they ask for it?

HELENA. Mr. Karonk!

MR. KARONK. (*moves to exit*) I was curious. That's all. Curious. I'll be out on the front porch, Dennis, after you've said your goodbyes. (*exits*)

HELENA. Dennis, I hope you don't mind.

DENNIS. Mind? No, no, why should I mind? Well. Well! This is my place now, isn't it? (*stamps foot*) Solid as a rock. Solid as a whole mountain of rocks.

CHARLOTTE. You'll be moving in day after tomorrow?

DENNIS. That's right. Day after tomorrow. Tomorrow's my college day.

MILLIE. (HELENA *pulls at* CHARLOTTE'S *arm, motioning her to stand up.*) College?

DENNIS. Agricultural school. Not exactly college. But I have to pinch myself everytime I—

MILLIE. But I don't understand. What are you studying? (HELENA *gets* REBECCA *to rise and exit.*)

DENNIS. Junk. Stuff I should know anyways. Crop rotation. Fertilizer. All the new gagetry that's coming out. And my father says—you see—Am I boring you?

HELENA. (*still with* CHARLOTTE) No, no.

DENNIS. Dorry put me up to it. Her brother took the class last year and all I ever heard since was: farming's gone scientific, what he learned, that class. Well. Here I am running on at the mouth.

HELENA. Millie. There's something Charlotte and I must attend to.

DENNIS. Oh, don't leave on account of me.

HELENA. Charlotte?

DENNIS. (*slaps his head*) Oh! Dumb me! I almost forgot. The reason I was coming over here was for the keys.

HELENA. I left them in the envelope. (*a gentle command*) Millie. (HELENA *and* CHARLOTTE *exit. There's a slight pause.*)

DENNIS. Helena really didn't have anything to do, did she? (MILLIE *shrugs her shoulders.*) All she did the minute I walked in was pull at Charlotte's sleeve. So. What do you think?—I'm back in school.

MILLIE. I'm proud. That's what I am: very proud.

DENNIS. How's Rebecca?

MILLIE. All right.

DENNIS. Millie, did you by any chance—I mean you didn't have to—leave any paintings in the house? One of me?

MILLIE. What makes you think Dorry'd want *my* work in *her* home?

DENNIS. Oh, Dorry doesn't know about us. Other than we were friends.

MILLIE. I see.

DENNIS. Dorry isn't very curious. Like this school business—I mean—What do you say, Millie? It doesn't have to be of me.

MILLIE. So we were friends. Brother and sister type friends, I imagine.

DENNIS. You imagine. (*pause*) Look. Forget about the painting. Maybe I should just take the keys. Then go help that man.

MILLIE. You've grown up. Matured.

DENNIS. Just turned twenty two.

MILLIE. I thought you were going to grow down.

DENNIS. (*shakes his head "No" but doesn't say a word, then slowly starts shaking his head "yes"*) All right. All right, all right. I didn't want to talk about us. I've got my own opinions.

MILLIE. I've got my own opinions too.

DENNIS. (*quietly, humble*) You didn't come to my wedding. I thought you could've done that. You know. And then I heard you stopped painting . . . just sketches around the house, Charlotte said. Well I thought you were going to New York. I really did. I saw myself as this stick in the mud. And you were going to—big things were going to happen to you. You were going to go places—New York, Paris. But you didn't. You're a stick in the mud now too, Millie. You haven't even left the county. I thought—I thought—so will someone please tell me—I mean if you and I are both sticks in

the mud...will someone please tell me...you know
...why...why...why I'm married to Dory....

MILLIE. I—I sent you a wedding present.

DENNIS. Goddamit, Millie. Goddamit why're you still
here?

MILLIE. Well. I'm leaving now. Wanna shake on it?
(offers hand)

DENNIS. You hurt me. Do you know that?

MILLIE. I hurt you.

DENNIS. Yes. Me. You hurt me, your friend.

MILLIE. (incredulous) I—I—Dennis—what are you
saying, Dennis?

DENNIS. You've acted like a little spoilt child.

MILLIE. No, no—I didn't hurt you. I've done nothing
but help you all my life, Dennis. Good god, you're the
farm boy next door. I've given you lessons, everything,
Dennis! And I hurt you? No! When Rebecca returned
from Nebraska, it was me—Millie—I—I got Helena
to sell the farm to you. Everyone wanted it. The
Bakers!—Everyone! Only I remembered how much
you loved this place!

DENNIS. Maybe I should just take those keys—

MILLIE. All my life I've done nothing but—And I
hurt you???

DENNIS. You're just lying to yourself. Can't you see
that, Millie? No! Helena came over, Millie! The night
Rebecca returned! And she begged me to take the
place. Cause she didn't want to bother. And she didn't
want to tell you. Cause you're still a child! Cause
you're so wrapped up in your stupid self! Well you
can't be a child for the rest of your life!!

MILLIE. TAKE YOUR FILTHY KEYS! ' (pushes
him, attack him violently) TAKE THEM AND GET
OUT OF HERE!! I hope you live in pain here! I hope
your wife—I hope your wife and fields are barren! I

hope you've nothing but misfortune here! (HELENA, CHARLOTTE *rush onstage.*)

HELENA. Millie! Millie, what's—

MILLIE. I HOPE YOU LIVE IN PAIN HERE!! (DENNIS *runs off*)

HELENA. Millie, control yourself!

MILLIE. (*hysterical*) How could you sell the house to him? How could you??

HELENA. It wasn't meant to be, Millie.

MILLIE. I can't stand any of you! (*moves to exit,* CHARLOTTE *stops her*)

CHARLOTTE. Dennis is married now, Millie! It's final!

MILLIE. (*struggles to be free*) You don't know anything about love! You're something dried up, disgusting! (CHARLOTTE *slaps her.*)

CHARLOTTE. I was Dr. Zeigler's nurse! In a very close room . . . with . . . Not *exhibited* like you! But I know! I'm sorry I slapped you, Millie. (CHARLOTTE *moves downright away from the scene, but does not leave the stage.*)

HELENA. Charlotte—

MILLIE. (*crying*) He doesn't even like Dorry! He told me! I hate Dennis! I hate Dennis and I hate myself! (*Rushes downleft away from* HELENA. CHARLOTTE, MILLIE *and* HELENA *remain onstage. The lights change abruptly, and we are into the next scene.*)

SCENE SEVENTEEN

(*There is no stop in the movement of the play.* HELENA *turns joyously.*)

HELENA. My sisters!! I've an announcement! I'm leaving this farm! No, no wait—I'm going west! *We're* going west!

MILLIE. With Samuel!

HELENA. Yes!

CHARLOTTE. How wonderful!

HELENA. We've got the tickets already! And we'll stop and see Rebecca and her child!

MILLIE. You'll see Rebecca!

HELENA. Yes!

CHARLOTTE. We'll have to pack things for her!

HELENA. And we've reservations to leave in two weeks!

CHARLOTTE. Two weeks!

MILLIE. (*kisses* HELENA) I'm so happy for you. And me!—another wedding in the house.

HELENA. Well, no. Not exactly.

CHARLOTTE. You've got the tickets? Where did you ever get the money for two tickets?

HELENA. My wedding present—from Samuel. He spent every cent he had!

MILLIE. But then how can you go? And *live* out there?

HELENA. I've saved a little. And he's still working.

CHARLOTTE. But what about Uncle Jacob—the estate. Really, Helena, this is all so quick.

HELENA. What about Uncle Jacob?

CHARLOTTE. We've got decisions to make. Are we going to give up life here and move to Manchester?

HELENA. I thought we'd decided not to go—to keep the farm and stay in America. Wasn't that it?

CHARLOTTE. I'm not sure. Everything's changed.

HELENA. Because we're going west?

MILLIE. Well, but of course. I mean you've got Samuel. Suddenly Charlotte and I, we're just—

HELENA. Precisely! I've got Samuel! So you must find something for yourselves. Sell the farm and the house. Move to Manchester! Travel through Europe! I don't care. Dine on veal and caviar for the rest of your lives!

REBECCA. (*offstage*) Charlotte! Millie!

CHARLOTTE. My god. What was that!

REBECCA. (*still off*) Charlotte!

MILLIE. That's Rebecca's voice! (*crosses to call out*)

MILLIE. Rebecca! Is that you?

HELENA. It couldn't be!

REBECCA. (*She enters upstage carrying a wrapped infant. Her sisters rush to greet her exclaiming "Rebecca!"*) Millie? Millie, I'm home! Oh, look at everyone! Charlotte! Helena! Everyone's here!

CHARLOTTE. But let me look at you!

REBECCA. (*crosses to set the child down*) Now wait a minute. She cried all the way home. And just now fell asleep. There.

MILLIE. She? It's a girl!

REBECCA. Of course it's a girl! What do you mean?

CHARLOTTE. Rebecca, let me look at her.

REBECCA. No, look at me! (*spins around*)

HELENA. Let the child sleep, Charlotte.

REBECCA. No-one's said anything about me! Homesteading, motherhood, it's changed me, hasn't it?

CHARLOTTE. No one bit.

MILLIE. Rebecca, I can't believe it. You look wonderful!

REBECCA. No, I've changed.

HELENA. Is this just a visit? One week? Two weeks?

REBECCA. God, no. A *visit?*

CHARLOTTE. Well, we mean did Peter—

REBECCA. *Please!* I'm so tired. (*moves from them*) The train ride, taking care of my baby all along.

MILLIE. But Rebecca—why have you come back?

REBECCA. (*tears*) *Because I love you.*

HELENA. But what about Peter? He loves you.

REBECCA. PLEASE! Please, stop. I'm so tired! Don't you love me?

CHARLOTTE. Rebecca?

HELENA. Of course we love you. But Peter loves you also.

REBECCA. Don't come near me! Helena, you sent the money! I hate you!

CHARLOTTE. What money?

REBECCA. The money for my farm. Only Peter found it. He said I tried to cheat him. He took it! Took it and put it on that worthless hole. That hole!!

HELENA. (*softly*) Rebecca.

REBECCA. DON'T COME NEAR ME! Oh, my darling, my baby—(*She runs to pick up the child. As she does so the blankets unravel to reveal no child. She immediately wraps the blanket into a bundle again.* CHARLOTTE *and* MILLIE *gasp.*)

HELENA. Rebecca!

REBECCA. (*crying*) You see—you've woken her. My darling, my baby. Everything's going to be all right. We're home now.

MILLIE. (*crosses to Rebecca, moves her to sit*) Oh, Rebecca.

REBECCA. (*almost inaudible*) Oats. Such a simple crop. But when there's no rain . . . what can you do . . . (*pause*)

MILLIE. What are we going to do?

HELENA. I don't know. (*Lights cross fade to evening.* MILLIE, CHARLOTTE *and* REBECCA *exit.* HELENA *moves to sit downstage center.*)

SCENE EIGHTEEN

(*We are on the back porch, late at night. After a moment,* SAMUEL *enters from stage left to join* HELENA. *He keeps his distance at first.*)

SAMUEL. Do you want to see me? I was just in the house and . . . I heard about Rebecca's return. I'm very sorry. How did the child—

HELENA. We don't know. Rebecca's still asleep. I just wanted to come out here and—

SAMUEL. And be alone.

HELENA. Yes. (*pause*)

SAMUEL. We're still leaving for California, aren't we—in two weeks. Helena, the minute I heard, you take responsibility, don't you?

HELENA. It doesn't matter.

SAMUEL. "Had I not sent the money. Not spent the summer with Samuel. All this wouldn't have happened."

HELENA. It doesn't matter who's responsible.

SAMUEL. What about her husband, her sister-in-law in Nebraska.

HELENA. But *I* could've done something.

SAMUEL. You could've interferred. That's all. But you couldn't have changed them. Or Nebraska. Or Rebecca.

HELENA. Rebecca? Rebecca played no part—

SAMUEL. Oh, yes, she did, Helena. A very big part. Nebraska isn't Lancaster county. The land here was cleared two centuries ago. But in Nebraska you fight—

HELENA. All I know, Samuel, is a child is dead.

Uncle Jacob is dead. My parents are dead. I'm only twenty-six! I'm young.

SAMUEL. And I'm proposing to share my life with you. (*pause*)

HELENA. Samuel, please, it's so cold out.

SAMUEL. (*He takes of his coat and puts it around her, holding her again. Then.*) Just think this through a moment. We could still leave for California. In two weeks. The situation's changed, yes, but Charlotte can care for Rebecca. It's just a slight change.

HELENA. It isn't slight.

SAMUEL. Helena, we could do it. Just one decision. We just turn our backs. And we leave.

HELENA. Samuel, Rebecca has just returned!!

SAMUEL. If you loved me—

HELENA. I'd never test you that way. "If I loved you, then I'd go to California." No. That's not it.

SAMUEL. But you would! If you loved me!

HELENA. (*desparate*) *I do love you!!!* And can we *please stop thinking* about California!!

SAMUEL. Well what else am I supposed to think about! Helena, you're pulling your family about you all the tighter. I can see it happening. Right in front of me.

HELENA. Samuel, Rebecca's just returned!

SAMUEL. And Rebecca's not your problem! Charlotte can take care of her!

MILLIE. (*offstage, as if very far away*) Helenaaa-aaaaa . . .

HELENA. What if you stayed here? Another month. Two months. We could leave then, just as we—

SAMUEL. Two months?

HELENA. Samuel, I'm here. I'm in front of you. And what is California?

SAMUEL. I've waited twenty-eight years. I've waited an entire summer with you. I can't wait any longer.

MILLIE. (*offstage again*) Helenaaaaaa . . .

SAMUEL. Look. I could wait for you. I could go to San Francisco and wait for you.

HELENA. No, Samuel. I'm not going to California on a—on a promise. I'm not—I don't know who these people are who go off to California! I don't know what they're made of!

MILLIE. (*offstage*) Helenaaaa . . .

HELENA. I'm on the back porch, Millie! I'll be in in a minute!

MILLIE. (*off*) Rebecca's *awake!*

HELENA. (*rising*) I'm going to sell the farm. I'll see Dennis tonight. He's always wanted it. And we can go to Manchester.

SAMUEL. You're imposing this.

HELENA. And you? (*pause*) Please don't come back. I'll take care of the men. (*suddenly*) Oh god, Samuel— bend, please, a little!

SAMUEL. I can't. I'm going. I've got to—

HELENA. Shh. Don't say anything. (*She kisses him lightly.*) I wish you the best . . . I give you . . . (*He exits.* HELENA *is joined by* REBECCA *who rests in* HELENA'S *lap. Music announcing another scene in the present. Lights cross fade to an interior.*)

SCENE NINETEEN

(HELENA *sits, right,* REBECCA *beside her. After a moment,* CHARLOTTE *enters.*)

CHARLOTTE. I was just walking about the house. Saying my goodbyes. It's so strange . . . looking out windows without curtains . . . rooms without rugs. Everything's so empty; when we'd filled it up so well. Mr. Karonk's nearly ready. I saw him from my bedroom window. She's asleep?

HELENA. Millie didn't mean what she said. (*Pause. After a moment*, MILLIE *runs on, carrying a large painting wrapped in muslin.*)

MILLIE. Dennis had already left. I thought to run after him. But when I got to the top of the hill— just as you see the Houser's farm—I stopped, out of breath. And looked down the path, and Dennis wasn't on it. Then I saw, just as my eye hit their home— Dorry swing the door open. And Dennis walk inside. I couldn't go on, you know. So I plodded back here. Look, I got thorns on my dress. And Mr. Karonk was tying things down. He wasn't happy about it. But I slid this out. One of my best, I know. But I'll leave it here. (*sets it down, then almost crying*) Charlotte, I'm very sorry.

CHARLOTTE. It doesn't matter.

HELENA. (*joyously*) We'll go to England! And we'll rest a bit. And we'll put Uncle Jacob's affairs in order. And in no time we'll be visiting Millie in Paris!

MILLIE. Or Rome!

HELENA. Or Rome! And Rebecca can—

MR. KARONK. (*Offstage*) Ladies! Ladies!!

HELENA. In here, Mr. Karonk!

MR. KARONK. (*enters*) Miss Helena. It's not that complicated. Karonk! K-A-R-O-N-K. People say it all the time.

HELENA. (*smiling*) I'm sorry. Karonk.

MR. KARONK. All right, ladies. Let's get a wiggle on. Up, Up, Up!

HELENA. Mr. Karonk. Could we just talk a moment?

MR. KARONK. (*sits*) Sure, sure. No problem.

HELENA. I mean—the four of us. Not the five of us.

MR KARONK. You want *me* to leave? (*She nods.*) Whatcha going to talk about? You're not going to talk about me, are you?

HELENA. Mr. Karonk, please!!

MR. KARONK. (*rises*) I'm just going to be outside.

Where'd you say you're going? Philly harbor? Yes-siree! You've got a new life ahead of you! (*exits*)

REBECCA. A new life.

MILLIE. I'm going to write Dennis. Postcards! Something public! I'll become Dennis and Dorry's travelling cousin. Aunt and godmother to their children. From Stockholm it'll be: "Opening! Raves! Three works sold!" In Paris, Monet'll kiss my hand and I'll write: "His beard tickled! Imagine that!" And then, old, skin dry, veiled in black lace, followed by a slew of spurned suitors, I'll come home. I'll come here. To this house. And at night they'll turn my bed down . . . and I'll sleep in my own room. (*She holds back her tears.*)

REBECCA. A new life.

HELENA. Twenty-six years.

CHARLOTTE. Quite a farm, wasn't it?

HELENA. Yes. Quite a farm. And it was difficult but we did it, didn't we.

CHARLOTTE. Yes.

MILLIE. (*crying*) You're all going to be utterly maudlin, aren't you? Well I've no intention of being— Oh, god, Rebecca!!!—Adieu, house! Goodbye, my rooms, my— (*to keep from crying she catches her first word and does a fancy curtsey*)—Adieu! Adieu! Adieu— To England! (*Sweeps to exit,* REBECCA *in tow. They move upstage and wait for* CHARLOTTE *and* HELENA.)

CHARLOTTE. Shall we go? (*music begins faintly*)

HELENA. (*takes her arm*) Charlotte, I hope our ship to England is a slow one. I hope there isn't one stormy day on board. We can sit out on the decks, four abreast, talking quietly, sea breeze across us. And each day will last forever. Shall we go? (*The foursome stands a moment. Music rises. Slow blackout. End of play.*)

PROPERTY PLOT

Scene six —
   bowl of raspberries
   artist's sketchpad and pencils
Scene eight —
   a letter
   knitting needles and a small ball of yarn
Scene nine —
   a small black bankbook
Scene ten —
   a large black account ledger
   wooden bucket with water and a ladel
Scene eleven —
   another artist's sketchpad and pencil
   small business cards
Scene twelve —
   a large blanket or quilt
   a wicker picnic hamper containing:
      a jug of wiskey
      a pipe, wrapped as a birthday present
      pipe tobacco and matches
   a large stage pillow
Scene thirteen —
   crocheting needle and yarn
   embroidery work
Scene fourteen —
   a blanket or quilt (left onstage from scene 12)
   a large stage pillow (left onstage from scene 12)
   two railway tickets in an envelope
Scene seventeen —
   a blanket wrapped as if holding an infant
Scene nineteen —
   a painting wrapped in muslin

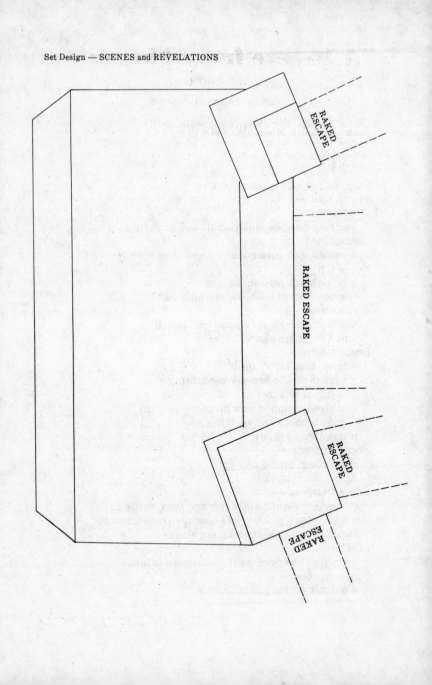

A Breeze from The Gulf

MART CROWLEY

(Little Theatre) Drama

The author of "The Boys in the Band" takes us on a journey back to a small Mississippi town to watch a 15-year-old boy suffer through adolescence to adulthood and success as a writer. His mother is a frilly southern doll who has nothing to fall back on when her beauty fades. She develops headaches and other physical problems, while the asthmatic son turns to dolls and toys at an age when other boys are turning to sports. The traveling father becomes withdrawn, takes to drink; and mother takes to drugs to kill the pain of the remembrances of things past. She eventually ends in an asylum, and the father in his fumbling way tries to tell the son to live the life he must.

> "The boy is plunged into a world of suffering he didn't create. . . . One of the most electrifying plays I've seen in the past few years . . . Scenes boil and hiss . . . The dialogue goes straight to the heart." Reed, Sunday News.

ECHOES

N. RICHARD NASH

(All Groups) Drama
2 Men, 1 Woman, Interior

A young man and woman build a low-keyed paradise of happiness within an asylum, only to have it shattered by the intrusion of the outside world. The two characters search, at times agonizingly to determine the difference between illusion and reality. The effort is lightened at times by moments of shared love and "pretend" games, like decorating Christmas trees that are not really there. The theme of love, vulnerable to the surveillances of the asylum, and the ministrations of the psychiatrist, (a non-speaking part) seems as fragile in the constrained setting as it often is in the outside world.

> ". . . even with the tragic, sombre theme there is a note of hope and possible release and the situations presented specifically also have universal applications to give it strong effect . . . intellectual, but charged with emotion."—Reed.

Other Publications for Your Interest

AGNES OF GOD
(LITTLE THEATRE—DRAMA)

By JOHN PIELMEIER

3 women—1 set (bare stage)

Doctor Martha Livingstone, a court-appointed psychiatrist, is asked to determine the sanity of a young nun accused of murdering her own baby. Mother Miriam Ruth, the nun's superior, seems bent on protecting Sister Agnes from the doctor, and Livingstone's suspicions are immediately aroused. In searching for solutions to various mysteries (who killed the baby? Who fathered the child?) Livingstone forces all three women, herself included, to face some harsh realities in their own lives, and to re-examine the meaning of faith and the commitment of love. "Riveting, powerful, electrifying new drama . . . three of the most magnificent performances you will see this year on any stage anywhere . . . the dialogue crackles."—Rex Reed, N.Y. Daily News. ". . . outstanding play . . . deals intelligently with questions of religion and psychology."—Mel Gussow, N.Y. Times. ". . . unquestionably blindingly theatrical . . . cleverly executed blood and guts evening in the theatre . . . three sensationally powered performances calculated to wring your withers."—Clive Barnes, N.Y. Post.   (#236)

COME BACK TO THE 5 & DIME, JIMMY DEAN, JIMMY DEAN
(ADVANCED GROUPS—DRAMA)

By ED GRACZYK

1 man, 8 women—Interior

In a small-town dime store in West Texas, the Disciples of James Dean gather for their twentieth reunion. Now a gaggle of middle-aged women, the Disciples were teenagers when Dean filmed "Giant" two decades ago in nearby Marfa. One of them, an extra in the film, has a child whom she says was conceived by Dean on the "Giant" set; the child is the Jimmy Dean of the title. The ladies' reminiscences mingle with flash-backs to their youth; then the arrival of a stunning and momentarily unrecognized woman sets off a series of confrontations that upset their self-deceptions and expose their well-hidden disappointments. "Full of homespun humor . . . surefire comic gems."—N.Y. Post. "Captures convincingly the atmosphere of the 1950s."—Women's Wear Daily.   (#5147)

SPOON RIVER ANTHOLOGY

CHARLES AIDMAN

Conceived from EDGAR LEE MASTERS'
'Spoon River Anthology'

3 men, 2 women—A stage

Via musical interludes, we are introduced in a cemetery to the ghosts of those who were inhabitants of this town, and whose secrets have gone with them to the grave. There are 60-odd characterizations and vignettes in this constantly interesting entertainment, offering an amazingly varied array of roles and impersonations, from young lovers and preachers and teachers, to the funny chronicle of the poor mixed-up Jew who ends up in the wrong cemetery. Both the sordid and the humorous sides of life are portrayed, with fetching ballads, and the free verse form of Masters. "A dramatic presentation reduced to its simplest terms . . . moving and beautiful . . . an evening of astonishing stirring emotional satisfaction."—*N. Y. Post.* "A glowing theatre experience . . . a brooding and loving American folk poem brought to life on a stage."—*N. Y. Times.* "Vivid . . . quite an inspiration. . . . A decided novelty. . . . It has punch and humor and bitterness, and often it stabs the heart."—*N. Y. Daily News.* "Warm, radiant, poetic. . . . A compelling experience in the theatre."—*N. Y. Journal-American.* "A procession of unforgettable men and women, and a powerful evocation of life."—*N. Y. World-Telegram & Sun.*

DAVID and LISA

By JAMES REACH

Adapted from the book by THEODORE ISAAC RUBIN, and the screenplay by ELEANOR PERRY

11 men, 11 women

The production is extremely simple; it is played against drapes and uses a minimum of props. The award-winning motion picture, *David and Lisa,* has now been adapted for the stage with the utmost fidelity to its illustrious prototype. It retells, by use of the most modern stage techniques, the strange, appealing and utterly fascinating story of the two mentally-disturbed adolescents: David, only son of wealthy parents, over-protected by a dominating mother, who is tortured by his mania against being touched; and Lisa, the waif who has never known parental love, who has developed a split personality and is in effect two different girls, one of whom will speak only in childish rhymes and insists upon being spoken to in the same manner. The play follows them during the course of one term at Berkley School, where they have come under the sympathetic and understanding guidance of psychiatrist Alan Swinford and his staff; follows them through exhilarating progress and depressing retrogression; follows them—and their fellow students: Carlos, the street urchin; the over-romantic Kate; stout Sandra, and others—with laughter and heartbreak and suspense.

Other Publications for Your Interest

A WEEKEND NEAR MADISON
(LITTLE THEATRE—COMIC DRAMA)
By KATHLEEN TOLAN

2 men, 3 women—Interior

This recent hit from the famed Actors Theatre of Louisville, a terrific ensemble play about male-female relationships in the 80's, was praised by *Newsweek* as "warm, vital, glowing . . . full of wise ironies and unsentimental hopes". The story concerns a weekend reunion of old college friends now in their early thirties. The occasion is the visit of Vanessa, the queen bee of the group, who is now the leader of a lesbian/feminist rock band. Vanessa arrives at the home of an old friend who is now a psychiatrist hand in hand with her naif-like lover, who also plays in the band. Also on hand are the psychiatrist's wife, a novelist suffering from writer's block; and his brother, who was once Vanessa's lover and who still loves her. In the course of the weekend, Vanessa reveals that she and her lover desperately want to have a child—and she tries to persuade her former male lover to father it, not understanding that he might have some feelings about the whole thing. *Time Magazine* heard "the unmistakable cry of an infant hit . . . Playwright Tolan's work radiates promise and achievement."
(#25051)

PASTORALE
(LITTLE THEATRE—COMEDY)
By DEBORAH EISENBERG

3 men, 4 women—Interior
(plus 1 or 2 bit parts and 3 optional extras)

"Deborah Eisenberg is one of the freshest and funniest voices in some seasons."—Newsweek. Somewhere out in the country Melanie has rented a house and in the living room she, her friend Rachel who came for a weekend but forgets to leave, and their school friend Steve (all in their mid-20s) spend nearly a year meandering through a mental landscape including such concerns as phobias, friendship, work, sex, slovenliness and epistemology. Other people happen by: Steve's young girlfriend Celia, the virtuous and annoying Edie, a man who Melanie has picked up in a bar, and a couple who appear during an intense conversation and observe the sofa is on fire. The lives of the three friends inevitably proceed and eventually draw them, the better prepared perhaps by their months on the sofa, in separate directions. "The most original, funniest new comic voice to be heard in New York theater since Beth Henley's 'Crimes of the Heart.'"—N.Y. Times. "A very funny, stylish comedy."—The New Yorker. "Wacky charm and wayward wit."—New York Magazine. "Delightful."—N.Y. Post. "Uproarious . . . the play is a world unto itself, and it spins."—N.Y. Sunday Times.
(#18016)

Other Publications for Your Interest

HUSBANDRY
(LITTLE THEATRE—DRAMA)
By PATRICK TOVATT

2 men, 2 women—Interior

At its recent world premiere at the famed Actors Theatre of Louisville, this enticing new drama moved an audience of theatre professionals up off their seats and on to their feet to cheer. Mr. Tovatt has given us an insightful drama about what is happening to the small, family farm in America—and what this means for the future of the country. The scene is a farmhouse whose owners are on the verge of losing their farm. They are visited by their son and his wife, who live "only" eight hours' drive away. The son has a good job in the city, and his wife does, too. The son, Harry, is really put on the horns of a dilemma when he realizes that he is his folks' only hope. The old man can't go it alone anymore—and he needs his son. Pulling at him from the other side is his wife, who does not want to leave her job and uproot her family to become a farm wife. *Husbandry*, then, is ultimately about what it means to be a *husband*—both in the farm and in the family sense. *Variety* praised the "delicacy of Tovatt's dialogue", and called the play "a literate exploration of family responsibilities in a mobile society." Said *Time*: "The play simmers so gently for so long, as each potential confrontation is deflected with Chekhovian shrugs and silences, that when it boils into hostility it sears the audience."   (#10169)

CLARA'S PLAY
(LITTLE THEATRE—DRAMA)
By JOHN OLIVE

3 men, 1 woman—Exterior

Clara, an aging spinster, lives alone in a remote farmhouse. She is the last surviving member of one of the area's most prominent families. It is summer, 1915. Enter an immigrant, feisty soul named Sverre looking for a few days' work before moving on. But Clara's farm needs more than just a few days' work, and Sverre stays on to help Clara fix up and run the farm. It soon becomes clear unscrupulous local businessmen are bilking Clara out of money and hope to gain control of her property. Sverre agrees to stay on to help Clara keep her family's property. "A story of determination, loyalty. It has more than a measure of love, of resignation, of humor and loyalty."—Chicago Sun-Times. "A playwright of unusual sensitivity in delineating character and exploring human relationships." —Chicago Tribune. "Gracefully-written, with a real sense of place."—Village Voice. A recent success both at Chicago's fine Wisdom Bridge Theatre and at the Great American Play Festival of the world-reknowned Actors Theatre of Louisville; and, on tour, starring Jean Stapleton.   (#5076)